POET STEALS HEADLINES

SENTENCED TO LIFE

Also by the Author

Poetry

Some Traffic
(Beyond Baroque Foundation, California, 1976)
Singing the Middle Ages
(Countryman Press, Vermont, 1982)
Traffic
(Harry Smith, New York City, 1985)
The Broken Iris
(Persephone Press, North Carolina, 1991)
Cow'sleap: a Nightbook
(Fithian Press, California, 1999)
Waiting on Pentecost
(Birch Brook Press, New York, 1999)
Trash: the Dahmer Sonnets
(Red Moon Press, Virginia, 2000)
Spending the Light
(Fithian Press, California, 2004)
Jack's Beans: a Five-Year Diary
(Birch Brook Press, New York, 2006)
From the Raft
(Verdant Books, Rutland & San Francisco, 2012)

Fiction

A Well-Behaved Little Boy
(STARbooks Press, Florida, 1995)
The Christmas Shopper
(Winner: 2009 A. E. Coppard Prize for a Long Story,
White Eagle Coffee Store Press, Illinois 2009)

POET STEALS HEADLINES

SENTENCED TO LIFE

Tom Smith

ReadersMagnet, LLC

Poet Steals Headlines: Sentenced to Life
Copyright © 2018 by Tom Smith

Published in the United States of America
ISBN Paperback: 978-1-948864-67-1
ISBN Hardback: 978-1-948864-68-8
ISBN eBook: 978-1-948864-69-5

All rights reserved. No part of this publication may be reproduced, stored in a retrieval system or transmitted in any way by any means, electronic, mechanical, photocopy, recording or otherwise without the prior permission of the author except as provided by USA copyright law.

The opinions expressed by the author are not necessarily those of ReadersMagnet, LLC.

ReadersMagnet, LLC
10620 Treena Street, Suite 230 | San Diego, California, 92131 USA
1.619. 354. 2643 | www.readersmagnet.com

Book design copyright © 2018 by ReadersMagnet, LLC. All rights reserved.
Cover design by Ericka Walker
Interior design by Shieldon Watson

Dedication

for Yvonne Daley

Acknowledgements

> "The world is so full of a number of things…"
> (Robert Louis Stevenson)

THE SUBJECTS OF ALL the poems in this collection are derived from a variety of tabloids and a few more respectable rags. These sources are credited at the end of the volume. The titles are almost always the headlines that accompanied the original stories.

Previously published are "Michael Jackson to Become a Priest" in *MARGIE* (volume two/2004) and "Liberace Ruined my Life" in *ATLANTA REVIEW* (Fall/Winter 2004) and *Vermont Writers: a State of Mind* (University Press of New England 2005) by Yvonne Daley. Also included in *Vermont Writers* are "Woman Finds Dead Leprechaun in a Jar" and "3000 Year-Old Mummy Pregnant." "Some Twins Are Accident Prone on Saturday" in *EDGZ* (Summer/Fall 2007). "Flatulent Sheep" in *KARAMU* (Spring 2009), "Dolphin Park Stirs Debate" in SEWANEE THEOLOGICAL REVIEW (Winter 2010).

Grateful thanks to fellow poet Joyce Thomas; also to Joan Houlihan and Martha Rhodes of the Colrain Poetry Manuscript Conference for insightful commentary and inspiration.

Contents

Schoolkids Scoffed at Nerdy Steven 11
Set Your Dreams in Motion 13
Flying Nun Vanishes Over Bermuda Triangle 14
Dwarf Stuck in Toilet Two Hours Tragedy at 20, 000 Feet 16
Amelia Earhart's Plane Lands/Skeleton at Controls 18
Flatulent Sheep Are Destroying the Earth 20
Where Are All the Robots? 21
Love Can Be Yours for the Asking on the 20th 23
Shrunken Head of Jimmy Hoffa Found
    in a Florida Souvenir Shop 25
Giant Squid Washes Up 27
Cast Your Net Far and Wide this Week 29
Liberace Ruined My Life 30
Ghost of Mom Haunts Wrecking Yard 32
Aliens Plan Visit to White House 34
Some Twins Are Accident Prone on Saturday 36
An Encounter with a Man Carrying a
    Ferret Could Lead to a Profitable Job Offer 38
I Allowed a Monster into my Life And
    into the Life of my Baby Girl 39
"A Lot of People Don't Know I Play Classical Cello" 41
World Church Leaders Conceal Last Day Prophecies 43
Man Shot and Killed while Pumping Gas 45

3000-Year-Old Mummy Pregnant Janitor Admits:
"I'm the Father" 47

Skirting Truth About Di's Duds Butler Wore Dresses 49

Human-Mouse Hybrid Experiments Stimulate Debate 50

Back by Popular Demand/World's Greatest Disasters 52

Operation Kuwaiti Field Chicken Shut
Down The Chickens Are Dead 54

Fish Talks and the Whole World Buzzes 56

Michael Jackson to Become a Priest 58

Woman Finds Dead Leprechaun in a Jar 60

Tyson Gets Warrior Ink 62

Listen to Foreign Words 63

Let the Captive Dove Fly 64

Lifelog 65

Angel Visits Hunter Who Shot Her
Gives Him a Message of Hope 66

Bizarre Creature Spotted in Louisiana Bayou 67

Boy Who Escaped Mass Grave Tells His Story 68

Celebrity Aries Assaults Paparazzo 69

Doctors Perform Tongue Transplant 71

Dolphin Park Stirs Debate 72

Hurricane Isabel Seen from
International Space Station 73

Gorilla Escapes from Boston Zoo 74

Beasts Are Blessed on St. Francis Day 76

𝖘𝖈𝖍𝖔𝖔𝖑𝖐𝖎𝖉𝖘 𝖘𝖈𝖔𝖋𝖋𝖊𝖉 𝖆𝖙 𝕹𝖊𝖗𝖉𝖞 𝕾𝖙𝖊𝖛𝖊𝖓

Inmate at Arcadia High in Phoenix, Steven
showed no interest in school or sports or girls. When even
his best friend ran off with a cheerleader, inviting,
>   "Come on, Steve, grow up.
>   What are you going to do,
>   make movies all your life?"
Steven lagged.

Kike, nigger, spick, mick, polack, kraut, wop, frog,
wasp, cocksucker, sissy, brain, creep, nerd.
They dubbed him nerd.
They dubbed him Spiel*bug*.
Scarab enchanter, rising sun.

A youth drags toward school, flopping his sloppy
mocassins along cracked pavement, rehearsing
sticks, stones, names,
knives, guns, bombs.

An angel appears waving pompoms, chiding,
>   "Come on, Jerk-off, grow up.
>   What are you going to do,
>   write poems all your life?
The youth sags

spilling out of socks and buskins
in the eyes of the world and heaven
nerdy, creepy, dull, queer, idle, dumb,
obsolete, irrelevent, determined
to create heaven and earth anew
in his own image.

Set Your Dreams in Motion

My life is a dream come true.
Only it wasn't my dream.

I have dreamed of flying over rainbows
on wings of burnished air, famous and invisible,
transparent as Hollywood or a bauble
in a morning dew. I have ached
to be Oberon like a star in the night forest.
I have danced in the rain
round all the sound
stages of the western world.
I have drifted with Huck and Jim down Mississippi,
with Orpheus down Hebrus,
with Cleo down Nile,
held the whispering asp to my apple breasts,
the general's pistols to my temples.
I have been Tut behind the golden mask
for centuries pretending to be dead.
I signed my soul away to Mephistopheles.
I took the shapes of plants and animals,
fire and water in Menelaus' grip.
I have dreamed Porphyro out of my closet.
I have sung to Sirens who have echoed
my Narcissus. I have been a golden ass.

Flying Nun Vanishes Over Bermuda Triangle

Hats off to Sister Inez!

In the company of professors and graduate students,
distant days of cocktail parties, saturation
of slow afternoons dissolving toward sundown,
I imagined myself floating toward the ceiling, wafted
upon a chatter barely distinquished from the clatter
of ice cubes in the cocktail shaker.
I might vanish like a cheese from my toes to the Cheshire
grimace stretched like a hammock between subversive dimples.

Sister Inez of the Blessed
Convent of the Bleeding Heart of Havana
adored the golden company of her fellows. Her walled
world of rosaries and rose gardens had no ceilings. The bliss
that brightened her brain, the ecstasies
that inflated her veins, the joys
that expanded her heart like Hindenberg lifted her,
love for her sisters in their dark
habits, love for the naked
God hanging above her, hanging before her, hanging
below her feet that paddled the liquid air.

Her sisters offered her to be an entertainment for Fidel
at the annual Mayday celebration. At sea
Inez should hover from one ship to another
like a visiting butterfly. Brilliant morning! She rose,
billowing black dot, toward the blinding sun.

She and the sun
one black illumination.
Gone!

Dwarf Stuck in Toilet Two Hours
Tragedy at 20,000 Feet

The toilet turned to vacuum.
The call of nature roared.
The night sky gasped
and all the stars inhaled.
He felt himself sucked into a maelstrom
to explode into the universe.

The stainless ring could only clasp his buttocks,
legs and torso jackknifed in the bowl,
crossed arms pinned between knees and chest,
shod feet clapping his ears where he kept
his head above water.

He called out, heard the echo,
heard the rattle at the door.

The stewardess would break in,
scream at the sight of him,
grasp his head,
begin to pull.
Someone would embrace her waist.
A third.
Another and another.
Tugging together.
Maybe

the commotion would send the plane into a spin
to spare him the embarrassment of being
rescued, the terror of being
uprooted like some animate turnip.

Amelia Earhart's Plane Lands/Skeleton at Controls

Have you scanned the skies?
I scan the skies.

Somewhere aloft
between New Guinea and Howland Isle
"at the height of the Great Depression"
Ms Earhart, Amelia…
suffered a grand elation,
locked hearts with her Lockhead Electra,
disappeared over Pacific deeps.
Howland and all the world
have awaited her return.

I fly with her. Invisible,
diffused through time and space,
we are water, atmosphere, and eyes.

We melt into a splashdown from the moon,
blossom like peonies over Pearl Harbor,
rise with the spirit of Magellan from his *Trinidad*,
watch with Noah the fall of Icarus,
fall of Phaeton who brings the sun
down with him.

The sun also rises. In its time
we have become metal and bone,
to bump down
on a decayed runway
in the world of eternal returns.

Flatulent Sheep Are Destroying the Earth

> "Farts Poke Holes in the Ozone"

Dies Irae…Agnus Dei… Baa!
"We are legion," say the lambs
as they frolic and fart in green pastures.

Vows Wally Macomber, shepherd,
"Some mornings you dasn't go in the barn without a gas mask."

Abel was the first shepherd.
The aroma of his burnt offering reached the divine nostril.
Abel was the first brother
after first born, first tiller Cain,
first killer, uprooted inventor of cities,
artificer in brass and iron, first smith.

The slain flesh of Abel exhaled its dissipation.
The ovine crowd grazed round and raised a mournful stink.

How history repeats, repeats,
repeats tiresome Cain
and tiresome Abel
and tedious old bugger God.

How it is always the end of the world.
How it is never the end of the world.

Where Are All the Robots?

> "According to the Robert Fursky Foundation,
> a Washington think tank,
> as many as 15,000 androids are hard at work
> in jobs across America."

How do we know
the teens who serve up mystery
meat and fries at McDonald's
aren't humanoid robots?
Our bank teller, with her odd hair lip,
may be an android.
Our home echoes with voices. "You have mail."
"Three messages." Our telephone instructs us
in the art of getting through, perfects us
in the knowledge of which buttons to push.
Do we believe these oracles are or have been ever human?

How do you know
the thug who mugged you beneath the bridge was not a troll?
Your coolly dispassionate rapist…not Apollo after all?
Patrol cars cruise the streets like UFO's.
Observe the hunks at the controls.
Do you believe mere flesh inflates
their deathless uniforms or packs
such sticks and pistols?

Do I believe in talk show hosts?
Their guests? Infernal trash,
the ghetto ghosts of the west.
I can hear the junk gears grinding.
How do I know Brad Pitt or Julia Roberts
eats, drinks, sleeps...*perchance to dream?*

I don't know
what pilots the plane.
I don't believe
we are the last of humankind.

Love Can Be Yours for the Asking on the 20th

I don't ask. I beg.

Take your love and fly it like a kite
or hyjacked jet to Cuba or Manhattan.
Let it drop like bombs
or the word of God
on the cities of the plain.

Feed it to cobras or rattlers
in Texas or India.
Let it drip from fangs
like acid rain on the brown
hills of Vermont.

Pack it away in a sausage
with anise seed and garlic.
Let it slither
off my plate
into my lap.

Lay it on scales
like a butcher's sly thumb.
Let it goose the air
like the national debt.

"Stay me with flagons,
comfort me with apples."
Take your love and shove it

up my heart.

Shrunken Head of Jimmy Hoffa Found in a Florida Souvenir Shop

Illustrious beheadings come to mind:
Mary Stuart, Marie Antoinette and her Louis,
Medusa hefted in the crazed grip of Perseus,
Orpheus' head singing down Hebrus.
Song has a way of looking back.

Lou Terkel, retired teamster, browses in his wife's
wake among bric-a-brac in the dusty shop in Miami.
Boredom rises round him like a foreskin which he sloughs
discovering the shrunken head on its brass stand. "Damn!
If that's not Jimmy Hoffa I'm a union-busting scab!"

Hoffa's notoriety began in 1957 when the Senate Select
Committee on Improper Activities in Labor and Management
found the International Brotherhood of Teamsters,
Chauffeurs, Warehousemen and Helpers of America
"racket-ridden, gangster-infested, and scandal-packed"
and denounced Jimmy Hoffa, its head.
I entered grad school in New Jersey.

Jimmy disappeared in Michigan. It was 1975.
I was newly tenured. We were ten years married,
nine and eight years parents, five years mortgaged,
two years sober, launched upon chartered lives.
We drift on the same sea still,
a polar bear couple on an ice floe in the sun
getting our heavy heads together over the grandsons.

About shrunken heads I can't recall any history or myth
and I don't know what Hoffa's pigmy noodle has to do with us.
But I do recall a joke told me when I was writing
sonnets for Jeffrey Dahmer. Query: What did the coroner find
in Jeffrey Dahmer's stomach? Answer: Jimmy Hoffa.

Giant Squid Washes Up

The creature from inner space approaches Tasmania.
Vacationers sprawl beneath a knock-out sun,
all about mid-afternoon in a hot and sandy place,
all about down under.

The great squid rolls through surf,
something the tide drags in,
morning-after party survivor
with streamers and sagging balloons.

He stands.

The sun-struck loungers stretch through lethargy.
A few sit up.
Somebody screams.

The cephalopod looms on two tentacles.
Eight tentacles search the inhospitable air.
He scratches what can only be his head.
He heads toward Gents,
a thatched shack under coconut palms.

A handful of adolescent surfers hang at the door.
The stranger finds the smell familiar though it isn't fish.
He washes his head and limbs,
splashing the warm fresh water,
coaxing slim suds from a sliver of Lava.
The stranger, humming *white tie, top hat and tails*,
observes himself in the cracked glass.

The boys make way.
The creature skims the sand, the waves.
He waves and sinks from view.
He sinks into the deep.

The surfers strain
to hear the limpid air.

Cast Your Net Far and Wide this Week

Scorpio stands in the shallow boat
and fans his net over the Mediterranean
mix of sun and salt, spangled mesh
fit for the flowing tresses of the goddess
who strides the sea swell.
Scorpio meets Aphrodite
on the cover of a Harlequin Romance.
Grand Union.

My wife and I stroll the air-conditioned aisle
between paperbacks and canned anchovies,
anchovies that
have flickered beneath the dimpled feet of the goddess,
floundered in the dappled net of Scorpio
where my brain lurks
amorphous as an octopus and hungry.

At check-out I contemplate *Globe, Sun, Star,*
National Enquirer, Weekly World News, New York *Times.*
I'm ready to chew that pulp and poop
poems that tread the water like a rush of fools
or surfers on the wings of angels.

Liberace Ruined My Life

He's forty-one, drug-free, living
with a girlfriend in Connecticut. What

were the rocks? What was the siren song?
The sex? Drugs? Diets? Celebrity?
Money? Jewelry? A gold Rolls-Royce? The plastic
surgery? The "hefty out-of-court settlement"? *Ruin*

is not a word that blooms much in the mouth.
The cheeks suck in on it. Lips pout.
Meanwhile, even as we listen to the boy

we are distracted remembering Liberace: his flesh
like gold leaf, his smile
like a grand piano keyboard, his extra-virgin pompadour
like the first pressings from a hillside grove in Tuscany, his hands
like birds of paradise or Zeigfeld girls
descending an ivory stair. He flashes

ermine and rhinestones and pearls, white velvet
tie and tails inside the studded cape that unfolds around him
like a night sky full of stars, an albino bat. How ridiculous

is the sublime! and how sublime
the ridiculous! What

a delicious word is *ridicule*!
Especially if pronounced with a little French accent, it froths
upon the tongue, strokes itself along soft and hard palates
like a cat against one's shins, fills the sensitive cavity
like a dog's tail wagging: *ridicule*! Every

thing

is so much more shadow than substance.

Ghost of Mom Haunts Wrecking Yard

Night dispatcher Kathy Henley gazed out the window,
grazed on her midnight brain. Saw me.
"Big blonde wearing overalls," she told reporters
come to crawl the precincts: public eyes couldn't see me.

The security video disappoints: only a white blob
making vaguely human gestures, giving a finger, giving a damn,
an oriole flourescence in a shadow coverall haunting
Pluckett's Wrecker Service Yard in Oklahoma City.

Our Ford pickup tossed me like cookies in the AM.
The Ford *tot*aled trying to climb a tree.
My German grandmother says *tot* to mean dead.
One death by motor vehicle occurs every twelve minutes.

My father and brother, my husband, even our seven children
swarm to answer reporters' questions. It's all about them.
They know I have come to comfort their doubt. They know
I come safe from some beautiful elsewhere to reassure their fear.

In fact, I amaze myself at my indifference to those people.
Except for the few who have crossed forgetfulness into oblivion,
we dead stretch everywhere around you living.
Don't worry about it. We don't worry about you.

I seek only to get back into that driver's seat.
What do you think I was doing? Out driving down the middle
of the night, a young woman with infant twins at home, a husband
at home, a family, a home. Where did I think I was going?

Aliens Plan Visit to White House

David Camp, insomniac of Waldorf, MD, staring at the milk
and cookies poised before him on the kitchen table,
2:00AM, heard fighter jets roar overhead. He ran
outdoors to witness "a bright blue flying object," American
jets in hot and hopeless pursuit. The object, says David
Camp, seemed less like a saucer than the spinning top
he played with as a child, his small hand pumping
the handle, the top spinning fast and faster. Betty
Bancroft and Martha Long worked late one Monday evening.
After dark, across the parking lot, they thought they saw
three children stretching and bowing beside Ms Bancroft's
Honda Civic. Three small figures skipped toward the two women.
Large heads and goldfish eyes shone eerie.
Dancing round Bancroft and Long, they touched at last the back
of Martha's hand. Promptly they disappeared. "Beamed up,
I guess," says Betty. Some Christmas cocktail-party
guests fell silent basking in a flood of unearthly light. Above
the Georgetown townhouse hovered a vagrant star.

Top secret Project Black Book concludes:
"The sheer boldness of the encounters indicates alien
visitors are close to revealing themselves very soon."

Across the White House lawn, skirting the Rose
Garden, some wee folk glide and giggle, giggle and glide.
A virtual sun behind them dazzles. They slide
down a beam in silhouette. Marines stand,
wood and cloth beside the doors. Snipers crouch,
tin upon the roof. The helicopter hangs above its pad

as if bagged in a catcher's mitt. The President
and some aides gawp at the windows, their brains
wiped clean of all the protocol so carefully rehearsed.
The visitors advance, prance, chirp like crickets,
a plague of Pleiades and fledgling spring.

Some Twins Are Accident Prone on Saturday

They turn away from their embrace
to rise from bed. They find themselves
sprawled upon the floor, the adamantine
floor beneath them, rumpled bed between.

Twin brother Apollo bemoans the prescience
that can predict only a burned toast,
a spilled or sour ambrosia,
misguided prayers of petitioners
"that cannot discern between their right hand and their left,"
even the quondam bastard presuming:
"Dad, can I borrow the chariot?"
pleading "a hot date."

Twin brother Apollo bemoans his butt.

Twin sister Artemis complains. "Prescience
is surely a pain in the brain."
She regrets the unintended victim
whose stare so startled her. He was damned
before she knew what she was doing,
his staggering fate sealed.
She blames the speed of light.

The divine pair rub their bums

and watch the empyreum crack
and crackle round them
as if they were pebbles dropped
upon the expanding surface of things.

Matter is accident
prone and so is anti-
matter.

An Encounter with a Man Carrying a Ferret Could Lead to a Profitable Job Offer

A maiden walking to St. Ives encountered seven wives,
a gaggle of gossips. The gang
divided like a marcelled sea
inviting her to their deep blue company. The damsel
caught sight in the dewy ingle of her eye
of seven husbands straddling tall weeds at the roadside.

A virgin climbing Pippin Hill observed a pretty fellow.
A stripling, a strapling, a sapling, a bud. He bowed.
She dropped a courtesy
and her pippin rolled down the hill.
The couple tumbled after.

A certain Jack led a spotted cow to market.
A stalker traded him beans for his sins.

As I climb the stair
I think a man.
He is not there.
Neither is his ferret.

Such present absence, Sir, enchants.
But keep your ferret in your pants.
I need not seek employment.

I Allowed a Monster into my Life And into the Life of my Baby Girl

Innocents can't help
but tempt and frustrate any monster's
lust, gluttony, anger, envy.

Zeus rapes Ganymede.
Cronos feasts on each baby son and daughter.
Jehovah despatches the first born of Egypt.
Pharaoh and Herod slaughter the new born of Israel.

Kings and gods ingest whatever purity impinges,
to make it their own, transform their sordid powers.

But sweetest flesh corrupts,
turns to shit, rots by the roadside
making stray dogs sick.

In Elsinore, California, Alejandro Avila exuded charm
disarming mothers and their small
daughters with whom he frolicked
in swimming pools, on swings and plastic
slides, all red and yellow, hot
in the seaside sun. Little girls
rode his pony shoulders up the stairs
to his blinded lair.

Embraces escalate,
entangle, strangle,
and five year old Samantha
poses unresisting on the hobnail
more like a flower than ever.

"A Lot of People Don't Know I Play Classical Cello"

confesses Chyna, queen of the wrestlers' mat. She plays
piano too. Plays late at night. Her baby
grand glows in the scented candlelight.
The photojournalist snaps, lurking beyond the fancy
candelabrum, catches her seated at the keyboard,
Debussy and Chopin in her fingers. She gazes
into the lens at you and me. She wears
only a ruby minidress. We imagine her bare
feet on the pedals. We imagine ourselves
pinned beneath those feet like pythons.

We think ourselves inside the camera
looking out at Beethoven between her knees.
He pretends he's a cello and they wrestle.
The music swells pulsing beneath her fingers
on his throat. Her right hand floats the bow
over quivering strings. She has been studying
cello since third grade she assures the interviewer.
I envision a prodigy with ponytail or braids and braces.
Photographer, journalist, you and I, we all
admire her white cotton jumpsuit with bell
bottoms and ruffled, peek-a-boo sleeves. Her right
breast peers round the shoulder of her instrument.
We observe the red lacquer on her left big toenail.

She is also pictured in the ring. She wears black
leather hot pants and bikini bra. At the end
of her raised arms, Hulk Hogan or some Ventura
wriggles on his belly. She looks about to spin
him on her palms. She stands
firm in her snakeskin boots' embrace,
boots that grasp her calves and twine
tight-laced toward her knees.

World Church Leaders Conceal Last Day Prophecies

> "Heaven and Earth shall pass away,
> but my words shall not pass away."
> (*Matthew* 24: 35)

The Pope sits on Ezekial, Matthew and St. John.
His cardinals also sit.
Hindu, Buddhist and Islamic delegations sit
upon His left hand and His right.

Seven seals now frolic on the rocks.
"The time of the end of all things is upon us."
Such old eggs may not hatch.

Here's an old woman. She lives in a shoe box.
She walks a cane between the bank and supermarket.
The bank cashes her social security.
The supermarket accepts her food stamps.
Somehow she is always broke and hungry.

Her husband and sons and grandsons are all dead.
There have been accidents in mines and factories.
There have been wars and AIDS and drugs.
Here's an old woman who looks into the sun
that blinds her to visions of war and famine.

She knows quotidian evils, commonplace of centuries.
She hears the angel singing, "Woe, woe, woe!"
She raises her cane against the empty air.
With any luck the words will pass also.

Man Shot and Killed while Pumping Gas

"Dear Policeman, I am God." The killer is always God,
but how many killers, or gods, hold the policeman *dear*?
The salutation chirps like a fledgling in tall grass
at the roadside contemplating its first flight, or a child
putting its small hand into the large hand,
which is probably gloved, of the tall man at the crossing.

The sniper leaves the note behind, printed
on the Tarot called Death. Death is the Roman
numeral XIII. In the pack, Death comes between
the Hangman and Moderation. The sniper comes
between heartbeats. He drives a white van.

God drives a white van that appears and disappears like a vapor
and becomes in its finally apprehended avatar a blue Caprice,
unholy ghost at a rest stop, the father asleep at the wheel, his ward
on his right hand, forsaken to the nightmare of the world.

God is an old soldier and, though the Military did
its best to teach him skill and etiquette, God is a sniper still. Death
don't discriminate. In two weeks' incarnation, God has achieved
worldliness. Death is costly. God is not talking obols: "Give me
millions." Death is necessary: "No child is safe." God grows
impatient, even angry with the *Dear* Police. God can't resist
the catechism: "Go to Alabama.
Seek me in crimes of violence,
find me in stumps of trees."

While a liberated people clap for the cops and leave cards
and gifts of pizzas and posies on the hoods of patrol cars, God
stands before the judge,
recovers good manners,
answers her questions:
"Ma'am? Yes, Ma'am."

3000-Year-Old Mummy Pregnant Janitor Admits: "I'm the Father"

Night watchman Dobi Sitar swings his light
to the left and to the right, foward and back. Its beam
carves brilliant, transitory tunnels through the darkness
of high galleries, wide passages, lofty alcoves, discovering
a shank of Sphinx, a thigh of striding god
or pharaoh, a golden arm extended, ankh
in hand, a golden solar disk, winged pectoral, falcon's
sharp beak of Horus, of Osiris or Anubis
the jackal's ears, alert, cat's eyes of Bast, kohl
enshadowed eyes of Isis staring
down the faltering shaft of Dobi
Sitar's torch, following down
the light to the night
watchman's fist that trembles with fear or anticipation.
The echo of his workman's boots on marble soars
into the darkness beyond his light, the high, wide,
haunted darkness of the National
Academy of Archaeology in Cairo,
Egypt.

Night watchman Dobi Sitar knows where he is going,
knows the way. He goes
to make love to death,
to enter dead flesh and bone,
to spill into the dark and timeless womb his light

and laboring echoes of his passion,
to cast a little slime of life like pearls
to feed the dead, to feed upon
the dead.

Night watches night. Toward dawn
Dobi Sitar wakes to climb a greying darkness
through the gradual, emerging splendor of antiquity. Bewildered
quickenings reach after him, well after him, sink back,
as Dobi Sitar thinks himself
back to the nursery of his desire.

Skirting Truth About Di's Duds Butler Wore Dresses

"Some day my prince will come."
The butler (Mr. Burrell) entertains
his fellow staff downstairs.

"The queen is counting the house,"
observes a footman (Marcel Proust).
Pudgy Peter (the butler) hikes a Dior hem
above his dimpled knees
flouncing French lace and winking back
at bitchy Marcel (nee Mark from Liverpool).

Two years' salary adorns his back,
caresses his dancing bottom,
flutters round his flesh like doves
or fields of ripening wheat.

Diana called him her rock.
But everyone gapes.

Pretty Peter bumps a hip toward a hooting scullion,
breaks his wrist over the congregation,
expects Scotland Yard.

He hurtles down dark Parisian rues,
crashing against the flashing lights
at the tunnel's dead end.

Human-Mouse Hybrid Experiments Stimulate Debate

> "A mouse with a brain made entirely of human cells
> would probably be discomforting to many people
> as would a mouse that generated human sperm or eggs."

Ubiquitous Mick and his Minnie.
Their offspring *chimera*
"mix two species of cells."

In ancient Greece and Rome the chimera sported
a lion's head, goat's body, serpent's tail.
Horace was one of the many people discomforted.

I fancy a mini-man with brains who's very sexy.
I laugh out loud when Max, a six-foot mouse, says, "Boo!"
Though science wishes to catch up with myth

some fantasies
had better not be realized
in fact, in matter, in matter of fact.

In myth, the chimera was slain by Bellerophon riding Pegasus,
Pegasus the winged horse of poetry born from the blood of Medusa,
Bellerophon thrown when he tried to reach Heaven.

In fable, mice are helpers. How else
would Cinderella make it to the ball?
The tailor fulfill his contract?

Mice in fact
chew your woodwork,
leave their feces in my sugar bowl.

As for people:
they cannot mind their own business, but
they can be toilet trained.

Back by Popular Demand/World's Greatest Disasters

Men, women, children strewn across a field of roguish grass
have drunk the blood of Jim Jones,
Kool-Aid laced with cyanide.
Mass suicide.

Remember the ant: "You sang? Now dance."
Union Carbide in Bhopal releases a cloud,
methyl isocyanate,
killing or crippling
400,000 little Indians.

Remember the grasshopper.
120 billion locusts eat
crops and wildflowers, bark off the trees,
clothes off the backs
of Israelis, Texans, Egyptians.

Misery drives cattle mad.
We live with it, even cherish,
in art, poetry, tabloid photography,
enbalm each pain or villainy.

Only time is unkind,
only the passing.
Memory only reminds:

We will not live again August 1945,
a boy learning desire.

Operation Kuwaiti Field Chicken Shut Down The Chickens Are Dead

With a handful of his fellows
Officer King creates
a burial ground with wooden crosses
commemorating Captain Popeye,
Lance Corporal Pecker,
The Unknown Chicken.

The chickens never saw battle.
No one knows why.
Officer King of Providence believes
they fell to their pecking habit:
choked on an unkind sand.

Whose eye is on the chicken?
Last summer, I noticed a white chicken who lived beside the road between Ira and West Rutland. Free-range bird, somebody's pet perhaps,

a solitary creature probing the roadside grasses and weeds,
sometimes on the north shoulder, sometimes the south.
I fretted about him crossing over.
He has gone missing since November. Roadkill?
He may have been somebody's dinner.
He may have wintered in a comfy rocker by the fire.
He did not fly south.

Nothing much depends on a white chicken.
Who hears me cry, "The sky,
the sky is falling…falling?"

Fish Talks and the Whole World Buzzes

> "I'm with you in Rockland."—Allen Ginsberg

"Enough already about the fish,"
gripes Mr. Rosen as he skins a carp.
Like the fish-wife who wanted to be God,
Zalmen Rosen has found out:
"A talking fish? Bad news."

In the beginning, Luis Nivelo, employee
at the New Square Fish Market, Rockland County, extracted
from a basket of ice, like a ninth infernal circle,
the fish in suspended animation.
Luis raised his club.

The carp began to chant:
>   *Tzaruch shemirah!*
>   *Hasof bah!*
>   (Account for yourself!
>   The end is near!)

Luis jumped back. "What's that?"
"The devil!" screamed Luis.
"*Meshugeneh,*" said Zalmen Rosen.

"Extra! Extra!" shout the newsmen.
Israel, London, Miami, Brooklyn calling,
Spanish-speaking rabbis, Barcelona, Madrid,
phones ring round the clock.
"Enough!"

After sleepless nights,
Mr. Rosen like a whisper
unlocks his New Square Market.
Mr. Nivelo slouches toward work.

Another day.
"It's called a living."

Michael Jackson to Become a Priest

Under the surgeon's knife the world lies dreaming
of wakeful beauty in high Catholic drag. It isn't
Diana Ross. It isn't Elizabeth Taylor. It's Michael
Jackson wafted upon an altar of chorus boys, flanked
by a chorus of altar boys, angels, putti, each white
superpellicium glowing afloat over neon dreamland.

And Michael's own white surplice unfurls like ermine
cumulo-nimbi unrolling round his fancied limbs and torso
and the tumble of black skirts, his cassock that gathers
like fog from which prim feet peer forth
over the rim of the dreaming world.

Michael's raised hands frame his smile
as he anticipates (as we anticipate)
an elaboration of vestments and accessories: amise,
alb and cincture, chasuble, dalmatic, humeral
veil, stole, pluvial, morse. Pyx or ciborium to contain,
monstrance to display the host. Gold and gem-encrusted
thurible exuding myrhh or frankincense.

I was never an altar boy but I did often kneel
before the peacock priest and his pigeon acolytes,
my sparrow brain dreaming to receive the host, my knees
naked and scabby, some buttons broken from my fly,
my short pants faded, and God on the tip of my tongue
like a word nearly remembered.

In the world's dumb dream of Father Michael,
the altar boys are faceless for no reason.
And in my recollection of any summer
Sunday morning I perceive at last we are all
faceless as a wafer, as white bread.
And neither wine nor water turns.

Woman Finds Dead Leprechaun in a Jar

Bridey Macabee faded to her knees through the breathtaking
attic heat, folded into a seated position on the silverfish slivered
floor beside an heirloom trunk in the act
of claiming her inheritance.
Her grandfather's old house whispered.
She harkened unable to shape any word.
She lifted the lid.

To discover (among costumes and paraphernalia, relics
of the migrant show, her grandfather once in Ireland ringmaster)
the old man's journal and a mason jar.
The ancestor's journal claimed a leprechaun
unearthed from a peat bog, nineteen aught four,
long drowned and preserved in those mystical
Irish waters.

The quart jar contained a wee man glowing green and no
bigger than a pickled pepper, grinning beneath the brim of a green
trilby, a rhinestone buckle on the band, and
matching buckles on the little dolly shoes, a grand
frock coat and breeches, also green, and candy
striped stockings.

Bridey Macabee observed that a leprechaun dead could not lead
her to buried treasure. Neither could he disappear if she
looked away. The fairy, she thought,
would make a curious display on the parlor mantel,
flanked by candles and framed snaps,
a family shrine.

At any midnight now, in the sleeping house, the wee
man in the wee hours lifts the lid of his left eye
and the dull orb sweeps the room in a counter-clockwise arc.
In his glass coffin, bored but not unhappy,
he contemplates good or ill fortune:
a gas leak, a four-alarm fire, a fatal collision,
a winning ticket.

Tyson Gets Warrior Ink

Mike Tyson glares tough inside his tattoo.
Supposed to identify the boxer with Maori warriors
the sign encircles his stare suggesting the dragon prows
of Viking crafts plowing the whale-road.
Or sickle moons in whose harbor
his eye rides like an evil star.
The opponent crumbles to sandstone before his gaze.

My dad too had a tattoo. Miss Liberty, all blue
and draped in rose-colored stars and stripes, rode
the length of his forearm, her swathed feet treading

the back of his hand

that sailed swift-like under the soft lamplight
as he swept cards into the invisible air.
I knelt against his legs.

My father's eyes were blue.
I basked in their snowbound glitter.
I traced Miss Liberty's flowing lines
with a nail-bitten finger.

Listen to Foreign Words

The lion's roar defines foreign.
His mane holds a language
entangled as the loquacious stars.
His pose and prowl express attitude.

The French have a word for it.
So do the Hindi, Russians, Japanese.
But their words cannot touch the lion's hoard
that lurks in his unabridged muscles.

I wish upon the stars to let me sleep.
The planets form a church choir,
but the stars make dinful gossip.

All the winds hang stalled in the trees,
silent and aghast beneath the scandal,
the folly that twinks the night sky.

We are advised to listen.
Were I a tree,
I would bark back at the stars:
"Scoffers! Scoffers! Scoff!"

Let the Captive Dove Fly

The dove has a short memory.
She does not remember descending
upon eleven men in an upstairs room in Jerusalem:
an affliction of tongues; she does not recall
riding the tide with the scandalous goddess; she forgets
the old zookeeper who tossed her across the flood.
The dove has no memory at all.
Still she comes home to the unknown shore.

I am the would-be skeptic
who can't resist a horoscope
taken with the morning cup of coffee,
forgotten before I've finished the crossword,
as I contemplate the tulip tree
outside the kitchen window lifting its shade
between me and the rising sun, visited
by cardinal, jay, nuthatch, goldfinch, robin.

I sip my instant brew and know
some crows patrol the edges of our lawn.

Lifelog

> "Coming to you soon from the Pentagon
> a multimedia, digital record of everywhere you go
> and everything you see, hear, read, say and touch."

In Soho, lower Manhattan, Henry David Thoreau
wakes to the woodland piping of birdsong from his radio alarm.
While Henry David collects his parts and begins to assemble
his senses, his computer Prince Hal recites
today's schedule, recalls
the events of yesterday, projects
upon the lofty walls remembered sights, injects
the air with sounds and smells.
A sensitive plastic membrane lines his oral cavity
and tastes as Henry David breaks
his fast, content that Prince Hal,

>   fed by cameras,
>   contact lenses thinner than communion wafers,
>   microphones and sensors (ears and nostrils),
>   tiny antennae sunk into every pore,

casts his existence broadly
across a World Wide Web:
double you, double.

Angel Visits Hunter Who Shot Her Gives Him a Message of Hope

Alabama wetlands. February wasteland.
Grey mosses hang shredded memories of war.
At half past a damp dawn where dank prevailed
Ted Sargo fired into a flock of ducks, brought down an angel.
The ducks quacked hosanna. The angel fell,
a large white platter, white Thanksgiving turkey
waiting to be plucked. "Hurl'd headlong
flaming from th'Ethereal sky." Ted Sargo
stood aghast on his flat-bottomed craft,
his smoking gun still aimed at heaven,
and watched Leviathan sink into the swamp,
sink like Titanic or a plugged nickel.

Alabama wetlands. May wasteland.
Ted Sargo returns to the scene of his guilt.
The angel ghost lifts off the hushed surface streaming mute,
perhaps mutant algae and wraith-like wispy mists.
She glowers, a bit pissed,
but remembers to don the benign smile of eternal dignity.
She needs no trumpet.
Sargo's *angst* provides a thunder.
Her arms raised, middle fingers pointing heavenward,
she addresses the cowering hunter.

"Love your neighbor, fathead.
Love yourself. Love God.
Love a duck."

Bizarre Creature Spotted in Louisiana Bayou

Alligator Man is lonely. His loneliness increases.
Alligator Man is hungry, sulks in a cramped backwater,
recalls in a cold fever his quickening
when a creature ugly as himself stomped through the bayou
pursued by his creator, drawing his maker in the wake
of mutual obsession. Two hundred years ago.
Such madness will not pass again; nor such understanding.

Alligator Man needs beautiful Mary Shelley,
her beautiful husband, their beautiful Lord Byron.
Only beauty shares the suffering of ugliness.
With the head and torso, arms and hands, of a man,
but a man scarcely more than his skull,
his skin hanging grey from his bones
like abandoned webs and dirt of old spiders;
in the end a reptile's knobs and scales,
his alligator tail dragging. Eternal and one of a kind,
his greatness is endangered. He starves
in the shrunken and polluted swamp.

Lately, however, marine biologists and convergent evolutionists
have taken up the cause of Alligator Man,
have tracked the creature down,
published their findings in *Science Monthly*, *Vanity Fair*.
With food and hideouts harder and harder to come by,
Alligator Man is promised fame and a career.
Steven Spielberg (mogul) holds the options.

Boy Who Escaped Mass Grave Tells His Story

"That kid isn't dead. Shoot him again."
The send-off. The last words spat.
Then came the rifle's thunder. Next came the dark.
First, because I kept my eyes closed tight and, after that,
the loose earth they shoveled over us gave very little light,
less air. I held my breath anyway against the facts.

Twelve years old. I held my mother's hand.
The soldiers pushed us off the edge of the living world.
I foundered among bodies, recently dead, long dead, or dying.
My mother lost to the smell and the darkness, my young
uncle and younger cousins heaped, maybe, above me,
beside me, below, anonymous meat and bone and blood.

No matter what the soldier said, I was probably a corpse
still thrilling to his echo and the rifles' boom, boom, boom;
still writhing, biting through the rags that bound me, treading,
rising, surfacing at last beneath the idiot gaze of the moon,
crawling upon the lunatic cold abandoned sands of Iraq.

Twelve years again have passed. I pass
among some who are living, and some
who imagine themselves to be living, and some
who believe I live among them. Believe me:
no one returns from his grave.

Celebrity Aries Assaults Paparazzo

> "Alec Baldwin…was taken to court
> for assaulting a paparazzo
> who had staked out the actor's house
> for shots of his newborn child."

The ram must lie down with the paparazzi.

The newborn sleeps
innocent of predictions,
forgetful of evictions,
in a peaceable kingdom.

The mother sleeps
adrift on a post-partum flood
awaiting the word.

The father paces.
The paparazzo crouches among shrubs.
The cosmos circles like a dog making its bed.

Murder hangs on the air
like a flashbulb about to explode,
like a front page byline.

Fame is the name of the game.
Fame is the game of the name.
The name is fair game.

When all
the names of the gods have been spoken,
when all
have been reduced to newsprint pics on foolscap,
then all
the stars will dim and whimper out.

Doctors Perform Tongue Transplant

The tongue hollers, "I'm out of my head."
I hear it like a thunder in my brain.

The doctors brag. "The patient shows no sign
of rejecting the organ." But the organ

(frankly I'd call it an appendage)
sounds very like rejecting me.

I'm feeling oddly depressed
missing the tenant tumor.

Does the tumor feel separation trauma?
How much did it love me, all

the potential chambers of my body it had yet to explore?
Now muscle and buds abandon me to the pain killers.

Those parts of me, tongue and jaw,
like family, with me since birth:

meat tossed in a bin, gone bad?
No wake? No rites of closure?

Which facet, aspect, joint, limb, tendon, loin,
lobe, bone, lung, liver, kidney will go next,

what cells explode inside the shell of me,
broken egg, piecemeal atoll?

Dolphin Park Stirs Debate

At Parque Nizuc, Cancun, in Mexico,
some people swim with dolphins.

The people are not Mexican;
neither are the dolphins.

The people have flown in
from Berlin, New York City.

The dolphins have been flown in
from Cuba, Solomon Islands.

In London, Gerardo Huertas, spokesperson
for the World Society for the Protection of Animals,

worries about the capacity of the marine mammals
to survive long flights and foreign waters.

Journalists, from around the world, tour Parque Nizuc
and witness dolphins sporting and dining.

A small boy sits on the sand beach
and weeps for home and his mother.

Hurricane Isabel Seen from International Space Station

The blue-veined, milk-white breast
of the Titan's wife pops
out of the *Times* front page
spilling over the dutch door
of the giant's castle.

Striding forth from the froth
of forty foot waves, the goddess
treads Carolina, Virginia, Maryland,
Delaware, Pennsylvania, New York.
Her wind-blown tresses waltz across heaven.
Her rime-sopping hem sweeps Canada.

Even our small village in Vermont
reels at her lunatic fringe. She strips
significant boughs off our white pines.
Lesser branches strew the lawn.
My tall plume poppies fall.
Isabel whistles down our chimney.

Gorilla Escapes from Boston Zoo

Little Joe
sits on a green bench
under a pink parasol
waiting for a bus.

Back at the Franklin Park Zoo his keepers pout.
What thought and expense they have put
to create an Eden for their charge, a tropical forest
exactly fitted to his needs and desires.
Still he ventures escapes, despite
hot wires stretched against his adolescent vagaries.
"How sharper than a serpent's tooth is an ungrateful gorilla!"

Far across town Little Joe
glows silver
beneath the light of a full moon
at which he points his parasol
while he idles at the deserted station.

From across the wide road I wonder:
where did he get the pink parasol,
where did he find white running shoes to fit,
how long
before the bus arrives to take him to west Africa?

Though the wide road yawns between us, we dream together
of a mountainside rain forest bathed in clouds
soft and moist as mothers' grooming.
Birds coo nearby and shriek in the hollow distance
that swims with leaves and flowers and butterflies
and no other primate exists
but us in the gateless universe.

Beasts Are Blessed on St. Francis Day

> "Did he who made the lamb make thee?"—Blake

A few cats have filled a moiety of my life.

Butch burst
my mother's back screendoor
and deigned to share
our hearth my world-war years,
a yellow tiger.

Lady gave me kittens on my nineteenth birthday.

Monsieur Le Coup crashed a Hallowe'en party.
The hostess sent him home with me.
We lived together (student, professor, husband, father)
thirteen years (New Jersey, New York, Vermont).

Dandelion exuded tapeworm.

We discovered my wife's asthma came of her allergies.
Everything furred or feathered takes her breath away.

I find cats breathtaking myself. Let me sing
their articulate flesh,
their fur that moves the breath of spirit upon the waters,
their animal life that rests with splendor,
their eyes that see everything, visible and invisible,
their arrival out of nowhere,
their presence eternal and passing as a vapor,
the joy they have of their burning.
Let me sing.

Sources

Schoolkids Scoffed at Nerdy Steven, *National Enquirer*, July 16, 2002

Set Your Dreams in Motion, *National Enquirer*, July 16, 2002

Flying Nun Vanishes Over Bermuda, *Weekly World News*, July 16, 2002

Dwarf Stuck in Toilet, *Weekly World News*, July 16, 2002

Amelia Earhart's Plane Lands, *Weekly World News*, July 16, 2002

Flatulent Sheep Are Destroying the Earth, *Weekly World News*, July 16, 2002

Where Are All the Robots, *Weekly World News*, July 16, 2002

Love Can Be Yours for the Asking, "Horoscope by Arlene Dahl" *National Enquirer*, July 16, 2002

Shrunken Head of Jimmy Hoffa Found, *Weekly World News*, August 27, 2002

Giant Squid Washes Up, *Weekly World News*, August 27, 2002

Cast Your Net Far and Wide, "Horoscope by Arlene Dahl" *National Enquirer*, September 3, 2002

Liberace Ruined my Life, *Globe*, September 3, 2002

Ghost of Mom Haunts Wrecking Yard, *Sun*, September 3, 2002

Aliens Plan Visit to White House, *Sun*, September 3, 2002

Some Twins Are Accident Prone, "Psychic Sarah" *Sun*, September 3, 2002

Encounter with Man Carrying a Ferret, "Psychic Sarah" *Sun*, September 3, 2002

I Allowed a Monster into my Life, *Globe*, September 3, 2002

A Lot of People Don't Know, *National Enquirer*, September 3, 2002

World Church Leaders Conceal Last Day Prophecies, *Sun*, September 3, 2002

Man Shot and Killed While Pumping Gas, *Associated Press*, October 2002

3000-Year-Old Mummy Pregnant, *Weekly World News*, October 8, 2002

Skirting Truth about Di's Duds, New York *Daily News*. October 23, 2002

Human-Mouse Hybrid Experiments, New York *Times*, November 2002

Back by Popular Demand, *Weekly World News*, December 3, 2002

Operation Kuwaiti Field Chicken, Ron Harris, *Knight Ridder News Service*, March 2003

Fish Talks and the Whole World Buzzes, New York *Times*, March 2003

Michael Jackson to Become a Priest, *Weekly World News*, March 18, 2003

Woman Finds Dead Leprechaun, *Weekly World News*, March 18, 2003

Tyson Gets Warrior Ink, *Sun*, March 25, 2003

Listen to Foreign Words, "Your Nostradamus Horoscope" *Sun*, March 25, 2003

Let the Captive Dove Fly, "Your Nostradamus Horoscope" *Sun*, March 25, 2003

Lifelog, *Associated Press*, May 2003

Angel Visits Hunter, *Weekly World News*, May 6, 2003

Bizarre Creature Spotted, *Weekly World News*, May 6, 2003

Boy Who Escaped Mass Grave, *Knight Ridder News Service*, May 17, 2003

Celebrity Aries Assaults Paparazzo, "Horoscope" Rutland *Herald*, May 31, 2003

Doctors Perform Tongue Transplant, *Associated Press*, July 23, 2003

Dolphin Park Stirs Debate, *Associated Press*, July 23, 2003

Hurrican Isabel, New York *Times*, September 16, 2003

Gorilla Escapes, *Associated Press*, September 29, 2003

Beasts Are Blessed, Rutland *Herald*, October 2003

www.ingramcontent.com/pod-product-compliance
Lightning Source LLC
LaVergne TN
LVHW020431080526
838202LV00055B/5137